Contents

Hadleigh, Essex

Work in the country

"I used to work along with the men, doing the same work, but I only got half as much pay."

50 years ago most girls and boys left school when they were 14. They went straight to work. If you were lucky you could stay at school until you were 18. Then you trained to be teachers, typists, and sometimes doctors, lawyers, artists or musicians.

Country boys went to work on farms or as gardeners' boys.
Some went to work as "boots" in rich people's country houses.

Look at the photograph above. The man and boys are sowing seeds from their aprons. The ploughman is ploughing the field ready for sowing.

"We used to go along in a crowd looking for work. Fruit-picking was hard on your back."

Women and girls worked
for farmers picking
potatoes, peas and
all kinds of fruit.
Look for:

— the man collecting the fruit. What kind do you think it is?
— the girl at the back who has been helping her mother.

Things to do

Start a book about work in the 1930s. Call the first page *Work in the country.*

Ask someone over 60 how old they were when they left school. What work
did they do? Write down what they tell you. At what age do boys
and girls leave school now?

Try to find out what work a "boots" did.

In the 1930s men sawed tree trunks into planks
using a two-handled saw.

**"The chap in the pit always had the worst of it.
He had to wear a cap to keep the sawdust out of his eyes.
It was thirsty work."**

Look at the man standing on the trunk.
He guides the saw while the man below keeps sawing.

"Some folks had tractors, but a lot of us preferred to use horses for most jobs."

Look at the men coming home from the fields with their horse teams. The horses had to be fed and watered and made comfortable for the night.

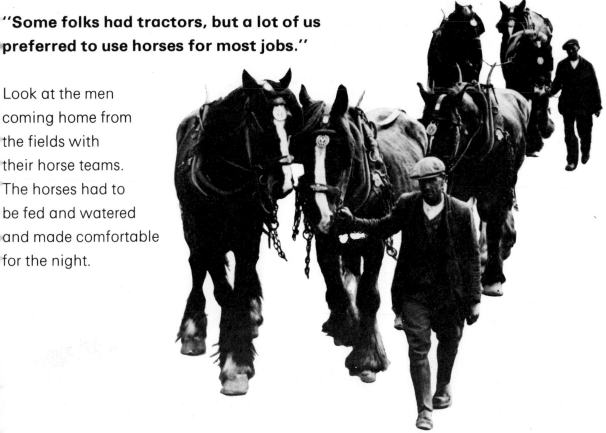

Things to do

Ask someone over 60 about farms in the 1930s.
If there is a museum near you, look for machines and tools which were used then.

Draw sawyers at work. How are wood planks cut now?

Would you rather drive a tractor or a team of horses if you had to plough a field? Why do you think fewer people are needed to work on farms now?

Helping hands

Some boys worked as
page boys in hotels.
These boys took messages,
carried parcels and
opened doors for guests.

Park Lane Hotel, London 1927

Lyons' Corner House, London 1926

**"I wanted the job because I got new shoes
and a smart uniform. We had to keep
the brass buttons clean. We wore our caps
all the time. When I got too tall I went
to be a boy waiter."**

There was no self-service in cafés. Waitresses
came to each table. Look at the waitress
in her black dress with a lot of buttons.
She was called a "Nippy".

**"We worked long hours those days.
My feet used to swell up. The customers
used to leave a tip under the plate."**

Many girls did domestic work. This meant cleaning and cooking in a house, a hotel or perhaps a hospital.

"I had to do the housework and then take the children in the park. When the mistress rang the bell I had to take the dinner into the dining-room. My bedroom was in the attic."

People liked to have a "maid" in uniform to do the housework and to answer the door bell.

Look at the neat uniform this maid wore. She is putting tea in the silver teapot.

Things to do

Ask someone over 60 what they remember about page boys and maids in the 1930s. What was a "skivvy"? Make a list of the work a maid might do in a household.

Draw a maid working or with the children in the park.
Draw a page boy in his uniform.

Work in shops

**"I was top of the class, and I really wanted to go
to the grammar school. But Mum wanted me to start work
and earn some money, so I got a job at Woolworth's."**

There was not much choice of work for girls. Look at the girl penned
in behind the counters. She is selling things you need for woodworking.
Can you see the price tickets? How much did things cost at Woolworth's?

**"I liked my work at the office. I thought to myself,
I won't tell anyone I'm married. I'll take off my wedding ring."**

When women got married they had to give up their jobs.
They were expected to spend their time working in the house.
There were no married women teachers.

**"I went to be a hairdresser
when I was fourteen. My dad had
to pay for me to learn. I got
no wages for three years.
We only had tips."**

A new way of curling hair was
discovered. It was called "permanent"
waving because it lasted a long time.
Look at the girl attached
to the machine. Electricity is
heating the hair which has been
damped with a special chemical.

Boys started work in barbers' shops
as lather boys. They soaped the
customers' chins ready for shaving.

London 1935

Things to do

Ask someone over 60 if they went to grammar school. Ask them about
Woolworth's in the 1930s. Write down what they tell you.

If there is a Woolworth's near you, look at the price tickets.

Next time you have your hair cut ask how hair was permed
in the 1930s. If you go to a barber, ask about lather boys.

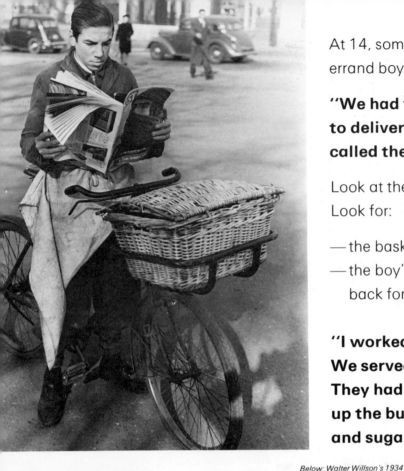

At 14, some boys went to be errand boys for shopkeepers.

"We had to go to the back door to deliver the meat. It was called the tradesman's entrance."

Look at the boy in the photograph.
Look for:

— the basket with a lid
— the boy's long apron folded
   back for cycling.

**"I worked in a grocery shop.
We served each customer in turn.
They had to wait while we weighed
up the butter, cheese, tea
and sugar."**

Below: Walter Willson's 1934

There were no supermarkets where you could help yourself. Grocers kept most of their goods on shelves behind the counter. Look at the assistants in their white coats. The tins and boxes on the high shelves were reached down with a grab on the end of a long pole.

"We used to have a little machine to make our own pills. There were no magic drugs like penicillin. It was always cold in our shop. We kept the door open all day in case of infection."

Law's chemists, South Shields, Tyne and Wear 1934

The chemist and his assistant in the photograph are "making up" medicines. Look for the pestle and mortar.

There was no National Health Service in the 1930s. People often went to the chemist to ask advice when they were ill, instead of paying to see a doctor.

Things to do

Ask someone over 60 about going to a grocer's shop in the 1930s. Who took the money? Was it hard work for the assistants?

With some friends, arrange a 1930s grocery shop. Stand behind the counter. Remember your customers cannot touch the goods. *Or* pretend you are a chemist, mixing medicines and making pills. Give your customers advice about how to cure their illnesses.

Work in the town

"We used to watch him pressing the pedal to turn the wheel. There were sparks when he laid the knife against the wet stone of the wheel."

In the 1930s most people used knives which needed cleaning and sharpening. The knifegrinder came round the streets with his barrow. He would call out or ring a bell so that you knew he was there.

Look for:

— the boys watching the knifegrinder at work
— the knifegrinder's name painted on the barrow.

"We used the hand cart to deliver milk close to the dairy. You had to be careful to balance it as you went down hill."

Most milk was delivered by horse and cart. Look at this photograph of a man using a hand cart. Look at the big wheels. The milkman has a heavy weight to pull.

Things to do

Ask someone over 60 about how often the knifegrinder came round.

Look for a knifegrinder's barrow in a museum.

If there is a dairy near where you live, ask about the 1930s.
Where did the milk come from then? Did it come in churns?
Was the milk all sold in bottles? What else was sold at the dairy?

Transport workers

"We had to get to work long before it was time for the train to start, to get up steam and to oil and check the engine."

Trains were powered by steam.
Look at the fireman shovelling coal on the fire.
He is heating the water in the boiler to make steam.
The driver is seeing to the engine.

Cheltenham Flyer 1932

"Sometimes the bus wouldn't start. I've seen five men pulling on a rope to get it going. It was all part of the job."

All cars and buses in the 1930s had starting handles. You had to be careful in case the handle "kicked". You could hurt your wrist quite badly.

Look at this driver "cranking up" his bus to start the engine.

London 1935

Things to do

Next time you go to a railway station, ask to see inside the driver's cab. How have things changed since the 1930s? Where is the fireman?

Draw a steam train of the 1930s and a modern train. Which would you rather drive?

Look at a school bus. How is it different from the bus shown in the photograph? Find out if there were buses where you live in the 1930s.

Working the coal

"I went down the pit the week after I left school.
I was put straight on to pony driving. It was very hot.
You had to put your lunch in a metal box or the mice would eat it."

Ashington Colliery, Northumberland

Some boys went to work down coal mines when they were 14.
It was dangerous work.

Look at the photograph of the boy and pit pony.
Look at the coal tubs on the rails.

"We had to collect the coal from the station. We weighed a hundredweight of coal for each bag. A big horse called Jumbo pulled the cart."

Sunderland, Tyne and Wear

Coal was delivered by horse and cart. The coalman tipped the coal into the coalhouse, or down a coalhole into the cellar below.

Things to do

If there is a coal mine near where you live, find out:

—what the big wheels are for.
—who looked after the pit ponies.
— how the miners washed the black coal dust off.
—what the miners wore.
Write down what you find out.

Why did the coalman carry scales on his cart?

Look at the chimneys near where you live. How many have smoke coming from them? How is your home heated?

Electrolux factory, Luton 1932

**"I did the same job all day long. If you went to the toilet
too often your pay was docked. One day the men sent me off
to get a pound of elbow grease. I did not know what the joke was."**

Boys who went to work in factories would sweep
the floor, make the tea and run messages. When
they were a little older they began to work
on the assembly line.

Look at the men making refrigerators.
Each one has his own job.

Ekco 1936

This wireless radio set was made in a factory.

18

**"I had a job once
putting the slit
in pen nibs."**

Some girls worked in cloth mills, potteries
or electrical works. Their nimble fingers were useful
for putting small parts together.

**"We had to work very fast. We had no lunch
in the workshop. There was no canteen.
It was too noisy to talk much. We used
to look forward to 'the pictures' after work."**

These girls are working in a factory that makes
razors. Look for:

— the girls working the machines
— the caps they are wearing
— the row of machines.

*Redox factory,
London 1935*

Things to do

Ask someone over 60 what they remember about factories
when they were young. Write down what they tell you.

See if you can find out about factories near where you live.
What factories were there in the 1930s? What was made there?

Look for an old wireless set. Draw it. Boys and girls may have
helped to make it. How is it different from a transistor radio?

"In 1931 they put in a conveyor belt. We had to work faster and faster. We had no paid holidays till 1939."

There was work to be found in car factories. The men had to work quickly to make as many cars as possible in a short time.

Look at the men rubbing the car bodies down ready for painting.
They used water to keep the dust from flying about.
There were no dust masks.

Cowley, Oxford 1930

Cowley, Oxford 1930

This photograph shows men working on the cars after they have been painted.
Look for:

— the men nailing the lining to the wooden parts of the car body
— the wheels of the gantry which carried the car bodies along
   so that each man could do his own job.

Things to do

Why do you think the men had to work so fast?
What is a conveyor belt?

Ask someone over 60 if they had a car in the 1930s. What make was it?

If there is a motor museum near where you live, look for cars made
in the 1930s. Make a list of the different cars. Draw one.

At the docks

Above: London Docks 1931

Dockers loaded and unloaded ships. They had to go to the docks every day to seek work. If a man was not chosen he had no work and no wages that day.

"The men used to stick their head forward and call out to the foreman hoping to be noticed. I've seen men standing for hours in the rain and then being turned away."

This photograph shows dockers in a ship's hold. Look at the hook the man is holding. It helps him to move the heavy sacks.

"I was a shipworker until I lost my job. In winter I used to hope it would snow so that I could earn a few coppers clearing the paths."

Jarrow marchers, near Bedford 1936

In the 1930s there were not enough jobs for everyone. A lot of people in the north of England, in Scotland and in Wales were unemployed.

In 1936 200 men marched from Jarrow, in the north of England, to tell the people of London that they wanted work. Look at the men marching in the rain. They are playing kazoos and mouth organs to keep cheerful on their long walk.

Things to do

Ask someone over 60 if they were unemployed in the 1930s.
Ask them about dockers 50 years ago.

See if you can find a picture of the inside of a ship.
Look for the hold where the dockers worked. Find out about container ships. How is the cargo loaded?

War work

In September 1939 war with Germany began.

**"As soon as war broke out there was a total blackout.
I had to do fire-watching all night at the office where I worked."**

Hounslow Barracks,
Middlesex 1939

Soon there was plenty
of work for everyone.
Women began to do work
which the men had done.

Look at these young men.
They have been called up
to go in the army.
They will soon be in
uniform.

The following museums have material about life and work in the 1930s:

The Museum of London, London Wall
North of England Open Air Museum,
   Beamish Hall, Stanley, County Durham
Museum of English Rural Life,
   Whiteknights Park, Reading, Berkshire
National Motor Museum, Beaulieu,
   Hampshire
The Science Museum, Exhibition Road,
   South Kensington, London

The National Museum of Wales, Cardiff,
   South Glamorgan, Wales
Museum of Transport, Albert Drive,
   Glasgow, Scotland
North Western Museum of Science and Industry,
   Grosvenor Street, Manchester
